In Viking Times

An all-year-round musical presentation with six songs and narration for scho

GW00720603

by Jan Holdstock
edited by Alison Hedger

Key Stages 2 + lower 3
Approximate duration 25 minutes

Besides singers, In Viking Times requires up to 30 children for short sections of narration introducing each song. The narrators are best dressed in costume. (If necessary, five narrators only will suffice.)

TEACHER'S BOOK
Contains the piano score, vocal lines, chord symbols, illustrations by Hilary Lack to stimulate ideas for costumes and some Did You Know? facts.

SONGS

1.	In Viking Times	*unison*
2.	Building a House	*unison*
3.	Chain Mail	*three parts*
4.	A Viking Town	*unison*
5.	Valhalla Tango	*unison*
6.	Viking Ship	*two parts*

A matching tape cassette of the music for rehearsals and performances is available, Order No. GA11037, side A with vocals included and side B with vocals omitted.

Pupil's Book Order No. GA11036 contains the narration, song words and choir parts.

© Copyright 1997 Golden Apple Productions
A division of Chester Music Limited
8/9 Frith Street, London W1V 5TZ

Teacher's Book Order No. GA11035

ISBN 0-7119-6223-5

The Vikings were energetic, daring, plundering Scandinavian adventurers of the 9th, 10th and 11th centuries who were bent on conquering new lands and taking anything precious for themselves. Their conquering success was due to good seamanship and purpose-built wooden boats coupled with steely determination and cut-throat aggression.

DID YOU KNOW?

• The name Viking means "bay-man" from the Norse word Vik for inlet or bay.

• The Viking understood and spoke a two-dialect Germanic language.

• The Vikings ate few vegetables and almost no fruit, but lots of cereals (rye, oats, barley and wheat), beef, cheese, eggs, deer, elk, polar bear, seals, whales, cod, herring, salmon and trout. They drank milk, ale, mead (fermented honey) and imported wines.

• The Vikings had spoons and knives but no forks, and houses with no windows.

• The Viking way of life was class conscious. Kings, chiefs and wealthy men were Nobles; farmers, merchants, hunters, retainers and craftsmen were Freemen; Slaves were the offspring of Viking slaves or captured foreigners. Class distinction was for life.

• A wealthy Viking was allowed several wives and he ruled his large family who lived together in one house. He had a special chair called a high seat.

• Viking women were not totally dominated and could air their opinions on various subjects, inherit property and wealth, withhold consent to a marriage (usually arranged by parents) and could even obtain a divorce.

• Viking roofs were slanting and made of turf, wooden shingles (tiles) or straw.

• Less rich warriors wore animal skins reinforced with bone and leather helmets.

Noble warrior   Ordinary warrior

• The Vikings believed in trolls, elves, giants, water sprites and the final destruction of the world. They had black magic wizards as well as priests and priestesses and believed in several gods.

• Vikings ships had a keel which reduced rocking motion and made steering easier.

• The Vikings developed a navigational aid to determine latitude by using a measuring stick and the sun, and they released ravens from on board ships to discover where the nearest land was. Hence the raven was the Vikings' favourite symbol.

Child 1   Hello, I'm Professor (*child's name*) and I'm an archaeologist. We can find out a lot about Viking Times by looking at things they left behind them.

Child 2   We go to a place where there used to be a Viking town, and we dig down into the ground.

Child 3   We have to be very careful not to break anything. Sometimes we use a teaspoon. (*holds one up*)

Child 4   And we use a paintbrush to brush off the dirt. (*holds one up*)

Child 5   We take lots of photographs so that we can show people what we have done. (*holds up camera*)

1. IN VIKING TIMES

Is there an - y ev - i - dence there to see— (*clap clap*) of Vi - king times?

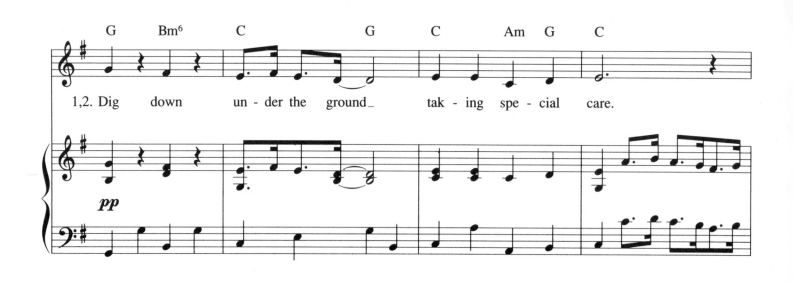

1,2. Dig down un - der the ground— tak - ing spe - cial care.

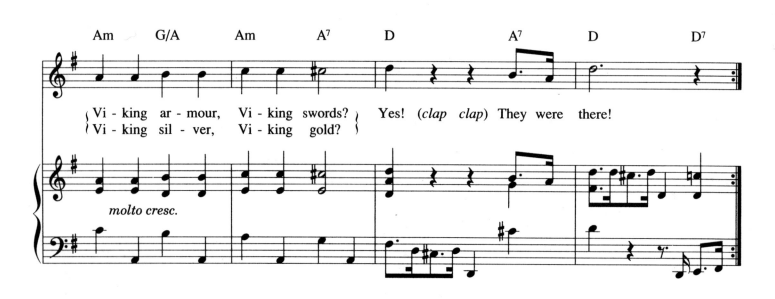

Vi - king ar - mour, Vi - king swords? } Yes! (*clap clap*) They were there!
Vi - king sil - ver, Vi - king gold? }

4

Child 6   I am Gest the builder. I use large pieces of wood to build the house frame. It will last a good 20 years.

Child 7   I help Gest. When the frame is made we get hazel canes to use for the wattle. We weave the wattle in and out to make the walls.

Child 8   I also Gest. When the wattle is all done we plaster mud over it to make the walls draughtproof.

Child 9   I am Jon the thatcher. I use reeds from the lakes and rivers to make the roof. When they are dried the carter brings them to the village for me.

Child 10   I help Jon. We put bunches of reeds over battens on the roof, starting from the bottom. We fasten them down with bent hazel twigs.

mother &
daughter

farmer

house
builder

metal
worker

merchant

2 BUILDING A HOUSE

Everyone needs somewhere to stay. Somewhere to sleep at the end of the day. We're going to build a

house that's new, and we'll do it the Vi - king way.

*F

1. Dig   four   holes   for the   cor - ners   to   hold   up   posts   of
2. Make   four   walls   out of   wat - tle   and   make   them   wa - ter -
3. Our   roof's   rea - dy   for   thatch - ing.   The   reeds   are   cut   and

wood.   Now   a   tim - ber   frame —   that's   good!
- tight.   Seal   them   up   with   mud —   that's   right!
dried.   Soon   we'll   all   be   warm   in - side!

Final Refrain

Ev - ery - one   needs_   some - where to   stay._

mf

* *to add interest, groups can take verses. Return to everyone singing for REFRAIN.*

7

Child 11   I am Erik the blacksmith. I work at the back of my house making things from iron.

Child 12   I help Erik. He heats the iron over a fire. I use the bellows to blow air onto the fire to make it really hot. I get very hot too!

Child 13   When the iron is hot, I help Erik beat it into shape with a hammer. We can make you a high quality sword, helmet and battle-axe.

Child 14   I know how to make chain mail. It will protect you very well in battle, but it costs a lot of money.

Child 15   I'm a wealthy Nobleman. I wear chain mail and a metal helmet. Naturally I'm very strong!

3 CHAIN MAIL

(part singing)

With strength ♩ = 132

1. Chain mail. What you need is chain mail. That will keep you

safe in bat - tle. That will keep you safe from harm. 2. Now put on your

hel - met. Now put on your hel - met. You'll be such a scar - y

sight. You'll give ev - ery - one a fright. 3. Pick up your

sword. Pick up your sword. May the gods pro - tect you in the

fight to - day.

div.

Play this section three times: a) verse 1
b) verse 1 & verse 2
c) verse 1 & verse 2 & verse 3

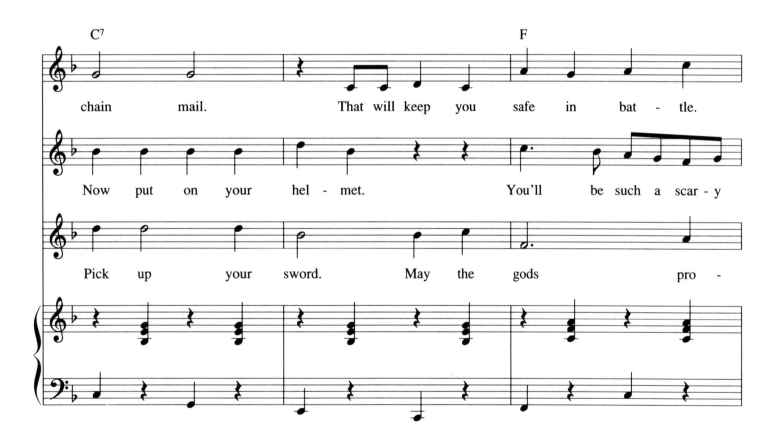

That will keep you safe from harm.

sight. You'll give ev-ery-one a fright.

- tect you in the fight to - day.

Child 16   I'm Olaf the shoemaker. This town is a good place to live because there are plenty of people to buy my shoes.

Child 17   I'm Ingrid, Olaf's wife. I like living in town because it has a good wall round it to keep us safe from raiders.

Child 18   I am Harald the Merchant. I have come to the town today to sell wine and silk. I've brought them from the lands in the south.

Child 19   I help Harald. When we have sold our goods we will be able to buy food from the farmers in the market.

Child 20   Our town is a great place to live — but watch out for the tax man!

4 A VIKING TOWN

With a swing ♩ = 88

Refrain

We like liv-ing in town.

Ev-ery-thing we need is a-round. Things to do and peo-ple to see. A

Vik-ing town._____ is the place to be.

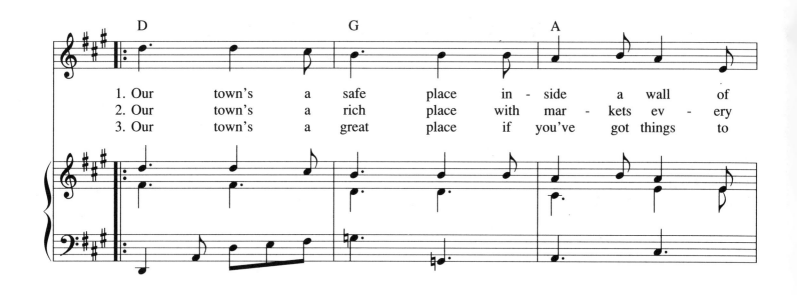

1. Our town's a safe place in-side a wall of
2. Our town's a rich place with mar-kets ev-'ry
3. Our town's a great place if you've got things to

stone._____ Our en-e-mies can't get an-y-where near so they
day,_____ for sil-ver and gold and won-der-ful things from our
sell._____ Get out in the street and set up your stall and you're

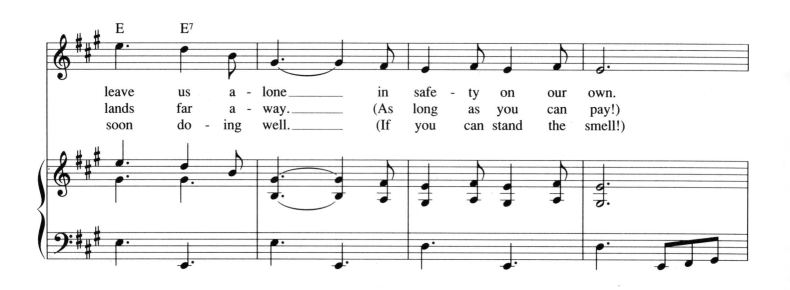

leave us a-lone_____ in safe-ty on our own.
lands far a-way._____ (As long as you can pay!)
soon do-ing well._____ (If you can stand the smell!)

Child 21 I am Odin. I am king of the gods and my castle is called Valhalla. It is a happy place, with plenty of food and wine.

Child 22 I am Thor, the god of thunder. Many tales are told about my mighty hammer and my great deeds.

Child 23 I am Brunhilda. If you die in battle I will send my maidens to bring you to Valhalla.

Child 24/25 We are the Valkyries. We will come on white horses to find your body on the battlefield. We will take you to live with the gods in Valhalla, and you will have everything you have ever wanted.

5 VALHALLA TANGO

Tango, positively ♩ = 100

I want to go to Val - hal - la___ up on a moun - tain high. I want to go to Val -

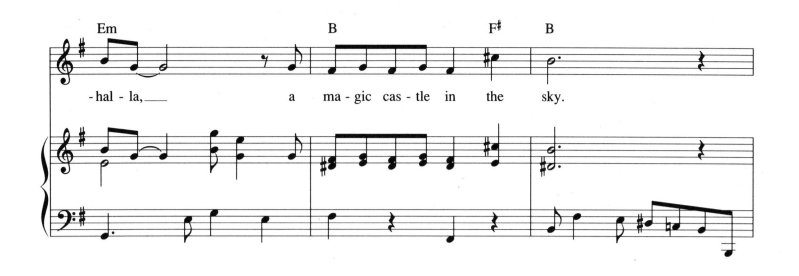

-hal - la,_____ a ma - gic cas - tle in the sky.

I want to sit in Val - hal - la_____ watch - ing the peo - ple down be-

-low. _____ And if I die in bat - tle, Val -

Child 26   I am Earl Thorvald. I have a fine ship, and I have a plan to get rich quickly. I'm going to attack a village!

Child 27   We'll row up the river quietly and take them by surprise.

Child 28   We'll steal all the silver and gold.

Child 29   We'll capture the people and sell them as slaves.

Child 30   Here we go!

6 VIKING SHIP

(part singing)

1. We've got a Vi - king ship, __ we've got a Vi - king crew. __ We've got a
2. We've got a dra - gon's head __ with ma - gic eyes to see __ your sil - ver

jour - ney to make,__ we've got a job to do.__ When the sun goes down at the
and__ your gold,__ where - ev - er they may be.__ And we need some slaves, so don't

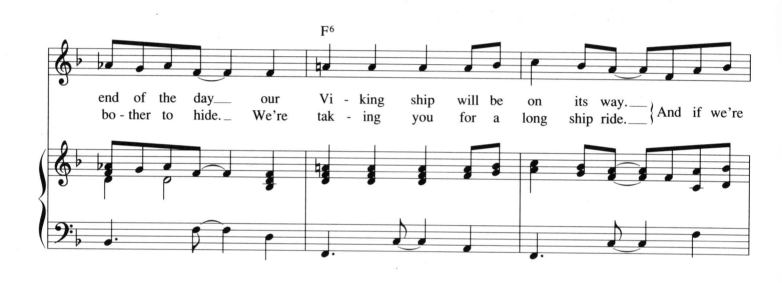

end of the day__ our Vi - king ship will be on its way.__ {And if we're
bo - ther to hide.__ We're tak - ing you for a long ship ride.__

head - ing up the ri - ver to you,__ what will you do?

Refrain

Here we go, pull-ing till our mus-cles crack.

Here we go, look-ing for a town to at-tack. When

we're com-ing your way then you know you'll have to pay.

21

looking for a town to attack. When we're coming your

Viking ship will be on its way.— And if we're heading up the river to you,
taking you for a long ship ride.—

way then you know you'll have to pay.

what will you do?

pay.

SOME VIKING GODS

ODIN God of wind and the chief god. He had power to see into the past and the future and he could change into any form. He rode an eight-legged horse. The alternative spelling of Odin is Woden, from which Wednesday is derived. Odin's symbols were the raven, the eagle and the wolf.

THOR A large, jolly, red-bearded popular god who caused thunder and lightning by riding his goat-drawn chariot across the sky. Thursday is derived from his name. His lucky symbol was a special hammer won in a wager. He was Odin's eldest son.

FREYJA AND FREY Beautiful twins who had power over all living things. Freyja was the goddess of love and rode in a chariot drawn by cats. Frey had power over the rain, sunshine and plants.

NJORD God of the oceans.

BALDER Odin's much-loved and popular second son. Every plant and animal vowed never to harm him, except the mistletoe.

LOKI God of mischief. The Vikings blamed Loki when anything went wrong.

(see page 3 of the Pupil's Book for illustrations of the other gods)

Mjollnir Thor's hammer

Odin's Raven

Thor

Odin

3/04(50168)
Printed in England